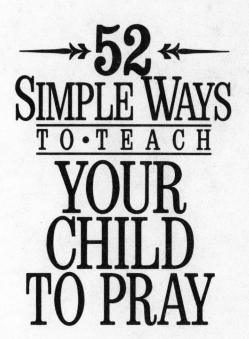

→52←
SIMPLE WAYS
TO·TEACH
YOUR
CHILD
TO PRAY

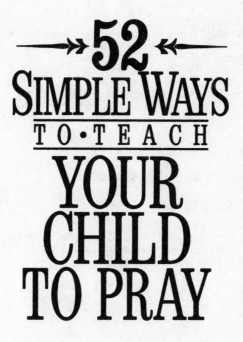

52 SIMPLE WAYS TO·TEACH YOUR CHILD TO PRAY

Roberta Hromas

OLIVER NELSON

A Division of Thomas Nelson Publishers
NASHVILLE

Published in Nashville, Tennessee, by Oliver-Nelson Books, a division of Thomas Nelson, Inc., Publishers, and distributed in Canada by Lawson Falle, Ltd., Cambridge, Ontario.

Unless otherwise noted, the Bible version used in this publication is THE NEW KING JAMES VERSION. Copyright © 1979, 1980, 1982, Thomas Nelson, Inc., Publishers.

Printed in the United States of America.

Library of Congress Cataloging-in-Publication Data
Hromas, R. P.
    52 simple ways to teach your child to pray / Roberta Parham Hromas.
        p.   cm.
    ISBN 0-8407-9590-4
    1. Prayer—Christianity. 2. Children—Religious life. 3. Christian education of children. 4. Christian education—Home training. I. Title. II. Title: Fifty-two simple ways to teach your child to pray.
BV214.H76   1991
248.8'45—dc20   91-9894
                                                                   CIP

1 2 3 4 5 6—96 95 94 93 92 91

Dedicated to

My cherished grandchildren who have heard the comforting words of prayer daily since before they were born. In the order they were sent from heaven:

Christina Danielle
Christopher Alan
Jonathan Michael
Joshua Robert
Rachel Elizabeth

Christina, seven years old, and Jonathan, four, sat down with me one afternoon as I was outlining this book and gave me two pages of suggestions about what I should write for you. We believe our grandchildren were chosen by God and sent to our family to nurture and train in His ways. What a privilege to love them and pray with them!

My heart is especially grateful to my mother, Pauline Parham, who taught me how to pray, so that I could in turn teach our children, Robert Alan and Lee Ann, who have loved and followed the Lord, and now they are teaching my grandchildren.

● Contents

Introduction

Teaching your child to pray is one of the most important things that you will ever do. Make it a priority in your life!

What is prayer? Prayer is the way God has chosen to communicate with us and to bless us as His children by answering our requests. Prayer spans the world and unites earth with heaven.

Prayer is talking freely to God out of the depths of your heart. It is truly heartfelt, soul-to-soul communication with our heavenly Father. It is communication that deepens, intensifies, and enlarges our foundational relationship with God as our Father. Prayer with other believers has the same benefit; we grow in our spiritual relationship with those who also love Him. No other form of communication will give your child more joy or fulfillment in life.

- Prayer is expressing to God your fears, worries, and concerns.
- Prayer is discussing with Him your problems, needs, and questions.
- Prayer is sharing with Him your joys and delights.

In teaching your child how to pray, assure your child that the Lord is *always* listening for your child's prayers. He is always available. Not only does He hear your child pray, He understands the motives and feelings of your child's heart. Not only does He understand, He responds—and always for your child's good.

Prayer is the most intimate form of communication that your child will ever experience. It is the one thing that your child can do that continually opens your child up to experiencing more and more of God's presence, His healing power, His joy, His unlimited love, and His impenetrable security.

Why does your child *need* to know how to pray?

- Prayer is the key to wholeness and to a feeling of total well-being.
- Prayer is the one thing your child can do that will have great impact on the extending of God's kingdom on this earth, no matter what other skills and talents he may have.
- Prayer is the one thing that your child will be doing on this earth that he will also be doing in heaven.

Make prayer spontaneous, free-flowing, and the natural, first response of your child to any experiences he has in life. In so doing, your child will develop the ability to "pray without ceasing" (1 Thess. 5:17). In so doing, prayer will become a firm foundation for everything else that your child ever does, says, or becomes.

And thus, prayer becomes the center of your child's entire life, the core of her spiritual being.

How can you best teach your child to pray? By praying! This book presents fifty-two simple ways. Use them as a beginning point. The more your child prays, the easier it will be for her to pray and the more she will learn about prayer.

In teaching your child to pray, you must recognize that *knowing* about prayer, *thinking* about prayer, and even *thinking up* prayers are not the same as actually praying. There is no substitute for the *doing* of what this book calls upon you to do.

Finally, we need to recognize at the outset of this book that, ultimately, your child will learn most of what he knows about praying by watching and listening to *you* pray. So, let your child overhear you talking to God. Be free to pray with, for, and in the presence of your child. Invite your child to join you in prayer. Pray together as a family.

And again, I encourage you . . . pray! You will never regret the hours of your life that you spend in this glorious pursuit.

1 ● Pray for Forgiveness

Have mercy upon me, O God,
According to Your lovingkindness;
According to the multitude of Your tender mercies,
Blot out my transgressions.
Wash me thoroughly from my iniquity,
And cleanse me from my sin.
—Psalm 51:1–2

Perhaps no more important prayer will ever be prayed by your child than the one he prays after realizing that he has sinned and, thus, needs to be forgiven by the Lord.

Parents often ask, "When should a child pray a 'sinner's' prayer?"

- When he feels a need to have his *own* relationship with the Lord.
- When he questions whether he will go to heaven.
- When he feels guilty about doing something that he knows is wrong.
- When the child is sorry for doing something and is afraid that he will do it again or won't be able to stop doing it.
- When a child expresses a concern about whether he has a relationship with the Lord.

That's the time to lead your child in this prayer or one similar to it:

Dear Heavenly Father, thank You for sending Jesus to die to take away my sins. I want to accept that gift of love that You have given to me. Send the Holy Spirit to live in my heart and take away from me all the things that I do that displease You. Please forgive me of all my sins. I want to be Your child forever.

Help me to learn more about You and to want to talk to you in prayer every day. Please give me a desire to read the Bible. I pray this in the name of Jesus. Amen.

Assure your child that this is one prayer that the Lord *always* hears and answers with a "Yes, I forgive you."

2 ● Praise God for Who He Is

Holy, holy, holy,
Lord God Almighty,
Who was and is and is to come!
—Revelation 4:8

The Lord takes delight in the praises of your child. It is your child's high privilege to praise the Lord for who He is, and to declare the excellence of His name! Teach your child about the nature of God by praising and worshiping God for the attributes He displays. Praise Him for:

• His almighty power.

Children understand the concept of "all mighty." God is mightier than all the armies of all the nations on earth. He is mightier than all the kings and presidents and prime ministers. He is mightier than all the ministers of all the churches around the world. He is mightier than any weapon ever created, any storm that rages in the night, any volcano or earthquake or roaring forest fire. God has all power, all might!

> *We praise you, O God, for your wonder-working power that is mightier than anything that the enemy of our souls might attempt to throw at us to destroy us, kill us, or steal from us!*

• His all-seeing eye.

Teach your child that God sees him at all times, day or night. God knows the innermost thoughts and feelings of your child. It is not possible to keep a secret from Him. His face is always toward us.

> *We praise you, O God, for your tender, watchful care over us and for seeing every detail, circumstance, problem, and joy of our lives!*

• His unlimited love.

Assure your child that God loves him. Nothing that your child does or says can diminish the love that God has for him.

> *We praise you, O God, for your lovingkindness that is always extended to us. Thank You for loving us, for creating us, for giving us life, for sending us Your Son to show us just how much you care about every part of our lives.*

• His eternal and available presence.

Assure your child that he can live with God in heaven forever and ever and ever and ever. Assure your child that God is available to him at any second of any minute of any hour of any day. God is in the moment; He is everlasting.

We praise you, O God, for Your presence with us today . . . and every day of eternity.

Encourage your child to learn more and more about God so he can praise God for more and more of His attributes. Make this your child's prayer:

Help me to know more about You every day of my life.

The more a child learns about the nature of God— through reading the Scriptures, prayer, and fellowship with other believers—the more your child will know all that God wants to be *to* your child and all that He wants to do *for* your child.

3 • Pray to the Heavenly Father

Our Father in heaven . . .
—Matthew 6:9

Encourage your child to address God as his "heavenly Father." Why? The number-one reason is that this is how Jesus taught us to pray and this is how Jesus referred to God. Time and again in the Scriptures we read where Jesus called God "heavenly Father" (Matt. 6:14, 26, 32; 15:13, 16:17, 18:35, among many others).

Second, children can relate to God as a heavenly Father, even if they have not had a good earthly father as a role model of fatherhood. They understand what a father is *supposed* to be and what a heavenly Father *can* be to them.

- "Abba," which means "Father" or "Daddy" in the original language of the New Testament, is One who *provides for and protects His eternal family.*

Share with your child the stories from the Bible that tell of God's provision, many of which can be found in the Exodus story: manna in the wilderness for the children of Israel, a pillar of fire for light by night and cloud of protection from the sun by day to guide them as they traveled to the Promised Land, victories over enemies that tried to destroy them. Assure your child that what

God provided for those "children," He'll also provide for them!

> *Thank you, heavenly Father, for giving me the things that I need. Thank you for keeping me safe and warm and protected.*

• *Abba (Father) is available day and night, forever and ever.*

Every child I've ever met wishes he could spend more time with his father. The heavenly Father is always available. He can always be reached.

> *Thank You, heavenly Father, that I can talk to You any time of the night or day, and anywhere I happen to be.*

• *Abba is infinitely capable.*

God, our Father in heaven, can be and do infinitely more than any earthly father can be or do. He is the perfect Father. He is the ultimate Caregiver. His love is unlimited. His patience is unending. His understanding and compassion are beyond measure. His abilities are unmatched.

> *Thank you, heavenly Father, for doing for me all those things that I can't do for myself or by myself. Thank you for sending Jesus to show me how You*

*want me to live my life. Thank you for loving me
even when I fall short of His example.*

As your child prays to his heavenly Father, he will
develop a concept of a spiritual family. As God becomes
more and more "Father" to your child, other believers
in Him will seem more and more like brothers and sisters. Give your child the wonderful gift of an extended
family that shares common goals and desires, a common outlook on the world, and a similar code of ethics.

4 ● Pray in the Name of Jesus

God also has highly exalted Him and given Him the name which is above every name, that at the name of Jesus every knee should bow.

—Philippians 2:9–10

Jesus. All authority in heaven and earth has been given in His name. And we, as disciples, friends, and His redeemed younger brothers and sisters, have been given the privilege of using His name.

● The name of Jesus is to be used only for good.

His name is only to be linked with that which is beneficial, healing, or a blessing to others.

> *Heavenly Father, I ask You in the name of Jesus to heal my friend of this flu. Take away the fever that is making her so hot and uncomfortable. Heal her upset stomach in the name of Jesus.*

● The name of Jesus is only to be used in a prayerful, respectful way.

It must never be used in vain or spoken flippantly. Using the name of Jesus is serious business. You are asking heaven to take action.

> *Heavenly Father, I ask You in the name of Jesus to protect us as we take this hike in the woods. Send your angels to surround us and watch over us. Keep us from all harm.*

I recently heard the story of a girl in China who was caught in a rock slide. Her body was so battered and crushed that her doctor covered her face with a sheet and had given up on her until he heard her whispering, "Jesus, Jesus." At that, he asked the nurse to clean her wounds. Much to his surprise, he entered her hospital room the next morning and saw her sitting up in bed, eating breakfast. He exclaimed, "The organs of your body were so mangled, how is it that you can sit up in bed and eat?" She said softly and reverently, "Just my Jesus."

The physician himself is the one who told me this story, and he concluded it by telling me that he had come to know Jesus as his personal Savior through this experience.

- The name of Jesus is to be used against the enemy —the devil, the father of lies—and not against people.

Discuss the difference with your child. We are to love people but not their sin. We are to value people but take a stand against the evil that may be manipulating their lives or blinding their eyes.

Heavenly Father, I pray in the name of Jesus that You would destroy the evil that is causing this person to be mean to me. Free them from the power of the devil.

As Jesus Himself said, "Whatever you ask in My name, that I will do, that the Father may be glorified in the Son." (John 14:13).

5 • Pray at Bedtime

And these words which I command you today shall be in your heart; you shall teach them diligently to your children, and shall talk of them when you sit in your house . . . when you lie down.

—Deuteronomy 6:6-7

Perhaps the most famous children's prayer of all time is "Now I lay me down to sleep, I pray the Lord my soul to keep. Should I die before I wake, I pray the Lord my soul to take." Unfortunately, this prayer is *not* one that brings comfort to many of the children who know it and say it. Bedtime is when a child's attention should be diverted to life, not death, to assurance, not fear, to goodness, not worry.

This is often the time of day when children are most likely to express to you their innermost feelings, thoughts, hurts, and concerns. They are eager to put down their own worries and fears.

Children often carry burdens they don't need to carry. They frequently hear just enough about an issue or a family difficulty to begin to worry about it. Encourage your child to use prayer as a forum for airing these concerns directly to God or to you in the form of prayer requests.

Beyond addressing your child's personal questions, problems, and fears, make bedtime prayers an opportunity for your child to:

• Give thanks for the good things of the day.

Thank you that I got to go to the park this afternoon to play with my friends.

- Remember family members in prayer.

Thank you for Mommy, Daddy, Ralphie, and Jenny. Thank you that Daddy got to come home early tonight. Please heal Mommy's cold.

- Ask for protection through the night.

Keep us safe in our house tonight. Help us to have a good night's sleep.

Include a prayer against bad dreams. Encourage your child to ask the Lord to guard his mind during the night hours.

Keep me from having any nightmares; let me dream only good dreams.

- Pray about the challenges of the next day.

Help me remember the right answers as I take my test tomorrow.

Tuck your child into bed with a hug, a kiss, and a prayer. Make it a habit. Your child will thank you for doing so all his life.

6 • Pray When You Rise Up

These words which I command you today shall be in your heart; you shall teach them diligently to your children . . . when you rise up.

—Deuteronomy 6:6–7

Teach your child to begin her day in prayer. Even before your child gets out of bed, she can say,

Good morning, Jesus. Thank you for today!

Set aside a time during the morning rush to come together as a family for prayer. It may be as you are finishing breakfast or just before the children head off for school or even as you are driving on the way to school. This is a good time to pray the Lord's Prayer together as a family.

Our Father in heaven,
Hallowed be Your name.
Your kingdom come.
Your will be done
On earth as it is in heaven.
Give us this day our daily bread.
And forgive us our debts,
As we forgive our debtors.
And do not lead us into temptation,

But deliver us from the evil one.
For Yours is the kingdom and the
power and the glory forever.
Amen.

—Matthew 6:9–13

Every child could know the Lord's Prayer by the time she enters first grade. There really is no more complete prayer we can voice to God.

In establishing morning as a prayer time, you may want to teach your child to "put on the whole armor of God," as presented in Ephesians 6:6–12. You can encourage your child to do this as she is dressing for the day. One way to instill the meaning of this concept into your child is to teach your child to say each piece of the armor as described in the Scripture passage and add a one-sentence prayer as she puts on a similar item of her own clothing. For example, as your son puts on his pants or your daughter a skirt,

I'm covered with truth. Help me, heavenly Father, to learn only Your truth today.

Encourage your child also to pray about any specific needs or challenges that he is facing during the coming day.

Lord, help me to do my best in school. Keep me in health and bring me home safely at the close of the day.

The problems may be ongoing ones. Encourage your child to pray about a problem each morning until it is no longer a problem. Recently a friend of mine had dinner with her five-year-old goddaughter, Laurie, who confided, "Nobody likes me at my new school." Laurie was feeling extremely alienated and lonely. My friend encouraged her to pray every morning as she got ready for school.

> *Heavenly Father, help the other children to be nice to me and to include me in their playtime. Help me to make friends.*

Within a week, Laurie reported back that two girls had asked her to play with them every day that week. She was glowing with confidence.

Many parents are concerned only that their children leave for school with sufficiently warm clothing and lunch money in their pockets. Be equally concerned that your children face their days with a covering of prayer and the peace of the Lord in their hearts.

7 • Pray at Mealtimes

Jesus took the five loaves and the two fish, and looking up to heaven, He blessed and broke and gave the loaves to the disciples; and the disciples gave to the multitudes.

—Matthew 14:19

Jesus recognized that all food comes from the Father and is worthy to be "hallowed" or consecrated by God for use in our bodies. Food sustains life; life is a gift from God; and our lives are precious to God. That's what a mealtime blessing is all about.

Use mealtime prayers as a way of teaching your children to recognize that God is the creator of life, the sustainer of life, and the provider of all that we need in life. One of the most ancient mealtime blessings is the gracious one from Psalm 104. It is often said by Jewish people today:

> *Blessed art thou, Lord our God, King of the Universe, Who bringeth forth bread out of the earth.*

You may want to teach your children a mealtime blessing that they can sing. Some families sing the doxology:

> *Praise God from whom all blessings flow. Praise Him all creatures here below. Praise Him above ye heavenly hosts. Praise Father, Son, and Holy Ghost.*

Another beautiful mealtime prayer song is this one taken from Psalm 145. It is often said responsively.

> *The eyes of all wait upon thee, O Lord,*
> *And thou givest them their meat in due season.*
> *Thou openest Thine hand*
> *And fillest all things living with plenteousness.*

Mealtime prayers provide three wonderful learning opportunities for your child:

• *Practice in praying publicly.*

The more your child prays aloud in the presence of others, the more comfortable he will become and the more fluent his prayers will be.

• *Practice in spontaneous prayer.*

A mealtime blessing need not be a memorized prayer or song. It can be a prayer that your child makes up on his own. Give your child the privilege of breaking away from memorized prayers to pray from his heart at mealtimes. It will be an opportunity for spiritual growth.

• *A time for recognizing that food is a blessing.*

We are exceedingly fortunate in this nation to have sufficient food to eat. Teach your child through mealtime prayers that food is a provision from God and that we must always be thankful to Him for our food and the resulting health, energy, and strength that come from it.

8 ● Pray as You Leave and Enter the House

Peace be to you, peace to your house, and peace to all that you have!

—1 Samuel 25:6

Very few things give a child greater comfort or a feeling of security than knowing that he is safe in his own home, and that his home is a place filled with the peace of the Lord. Strive to make your home such a place.

Peace is a state that comes about when the heavenly Father is invited to dwell within. Make that a part of your child's prayer life.

Heavenly Father, we invite you to live in our home with us. We invite you to live in the heart of each member of our family.

Peace reigns in a home when family members have a relationship marked by forgiveness and forbearance. Make those traits a matter of prayer, too.

Heavenly Father, please help us to forgive one another when we get on each other's nerves or when we hurt one another. Help us to be patient and kind to one another. Help us to say 'I'm sorry' and to mean it when we do something wrong to one another.

As your children come and go from your peaceful home, encourage them to pray for two things:

• *Personal protection.*

A child is often braver in facing life's challenges when his attention is called to the fact that a safe haven awaits him at the day's end.

• *Personal blessing.*

Encourage your child to share with others the presence of the Lord that she experiences in your home.

As you leave your home on vacations, pray that the Lord will guard your home against intruders until you return.

For centuries, Jewish people have attached a small mezuzah to the doorposts of their homes. It is a small piece of parchment inscribed with passages from Deuteronomy, then rolled and put into a case. The mezuzah represents the Law to them, which Moses taught them they were to "write . . . on the doorposts of your house and on your gates" (Deut. 6:9). As they enter their homes, the orthodox Jews kiss their fingertips and then touch the mezuzah. It is a way of acknowledging their arrival into a place sacred to the Lord and set apart for His presence.

9 • Nothing Is Too Small for Prayer

Are not two sparrows sold for a copper coin? And not one of them falls to the ground apart from your Father's will. But the very hairs of your head are all numbered. Do not fear therefore; you are of more value than many sparrows.

—Matthew 10:29–31

From the time your child begins to understand language, he is told in numerous ways that he is "little." How comforting to a child to know that nothing is too little for God's notice—including little children!

God sees every bird flying in the sky. He knows about every hair on your child's head. And if God knows that, as Jesus Christ taught, then surely God knows when your child:

- *falls off her bicycle;*
- *faces a strange dog in the neighborhood;*
- *rides his skateboard down a hill that is too steep;*
- *has a friend who says something that hurts his feelings;*
- *is excluded from a game.*

Let your child know that he can pray about each accident, mistake, hurt, problem, and embarrassment in his life. God also takes note of:

- *Every kind compliment or word of encouragement your child gives to others;*
- *your child's helpful deeds;*
- *your child's accomplishments and victories; and*
- *every word of praise uttered by your child!*

God is always listening. Indeed, God is eager to hear your child talk to Him about anything and everything.

As you take a walk with your child through a park, make note of the small things that God is seeing, even as you are seeing them.

- Praise Him for the beautiful butterflies that speak to us of God's resurrection power.
- Thank Him for the tiny pebbles in the stream that cause the water to splash and purify itself.
- Notice that it is the leaves of a tree, each one of them quite small, that give life to the tree.
- Watch the insects at work and thank God for the lesson they give, that God has ordered all of creation, with each creature given a specific role and function to fill.

Don't let your children reserve God for big moments, big decisions, or big ceremonies. Create in your child an awareness that God is in every detail and every minute, and that prayer is appropriate for small issues as well as large ones.

10 • Nothing Is Too Big for Prayer

Behold, I am the Lord, the God of all flesh. Is there anything too hard for Me?
—Jeremiah 32:26

The physical age of a person has very little to do with spiritual capacity or "faith power." Adults may have anemic, underdeveloped, or atrophied faith. Teach your child that he has been given a measure of faith; encourage your child to grow in faith by praying and believing for the hand of God to move on his behalf—even for big miracles!

Danny, a personal family friend, experienced the power of prayer when he was a teenager. While running backwards on a basketball court during a series of drills, Danny fell and broke his arm. An X-ray confirmed the break in the femur. The attending physician told Danny that he would need to put a cast on the arm and that he would not be able to resume his basketball career for at least six weeks. A major game was coming up in two weeks.

Danny's mother, Judy, had been listening to a sermon about healing before the accident happened, and when the doctor left the examining room Danny and Judy began to pray together for a complete and rapid healing of Danny's arm. When the physician returned, Judy and Danny asked that only a soft cast be put on his arm. He reluctantly agreed, with the provision that Danny would return in a day or so and be examined again.

After leaving the doctor's office, Danny and his mother proceeded to a friend's house, where the group read scriptures related to healing, laid hands on Danny and prayed, and partook of Communion together.

Several days passed and the coach kept Danny on the bench during basketball practices. Danny told his coach, "God cares about all of my life, including basketball. He knows how much I want to play and He's healed my arm. I know He has!" Danny returned to the doctor and had a second X-ray. It confirmed what Danny already knew—the break had healed completely. Danny was able to play in the championship game as he had hoped!

"But what if my child doesn't experience a miracle or see an answer from God?" you may ask. "Won't that destroy his faith or cause him to be discouraged in his relationship with God?" No, not if you teach your child one simple but vital fact about prayer. It is *our* responsibility to pray and to believe and to ask God for the desires of our heart. It is *God's* responsibility to answer our prayers according to His wisdom.

We can't do God's part and He won't do ours. Furthermore, God wants us to ask. The prime reason for your child to pray is to give God the opportunity to work as He wills.

11 ● Sometimes God Says Yes

So I say to you, ask, and it will be given to you; seek, and you will find; knock, and it will be opened to you.

—Luke 11:9

Some people seem afraid to ask God for things because they fear He will say no. Try taking the opposite approach. Ask God for things because He may very well say yes!

Teach your child that God sees our requests in the total context of our lives. He knows the beginning from the ending. He knows us far better than we know ourselves. He knows our weaknesses and our strengths. He knows what will make us happy and what will make us sad. He knows what is good for us.

Teach your child to pray,

> *God, you know everything about me. You know what is right for me. I want [petition]. If it's OK with You for me to have that, I'd sure like it!*

Assure your child that God only wants what is good for his or her total well-being. Teach your child to pray,

> *Heavenly Father, I want your best for my life. You know what that is. Please send it my way.*

Let your child be bold in asking for what he needs.

Heavenly Father, I ask You to heal me. I ask you to keep me safe . . . to provide enough food and water for me . . . to give me warmth when it's cold and cool shelter when it's hot.

Encourage your child to ask for spiritual blessings.

Heavenly Father, I want to feel more of Your presence. I want to experience Your love for me. I want to be assured You are always there for me. I want Your forgiveness . . . Your guidance . . . Your wisdom . . . Your compassion.

Give your child permission to ask God for things that give him or her pleasure. Teach your child that the heavenly Father experiences joy in what causes us to feel joy!

Encourage your child to ask God for the things he wants, not only for the things he needs. Your child may well discover that God says yes far more than He says no.

12 • Sometimes God Says No

"For My thoughts are not your thoughts,
Nor are your ways My ways," says the Lord.
"For as the heavens are higher than the earth,
So are My ways higher than your ways,
And My thoughts than your thoughts."
—Isaiah 55:9

We don't know all of the reasons that God doesn't answer our prayers with the answers that we want. But we do know some of the reasons, and you can explain these reasons to your child.

- God sees our entire life. He will not give us something now that may lead to harm later in our life, or in eternity.
- God not only sees our lives but the lives of all around us. He will never give us something that might cause harm to someone else.
- God sees our weaknesses. He will not give us something that makes us weaker still.
- Above all, God has a purpose and a reason even when He says no.

Does that mean we should stop asking of God? No! We still have the privilege to ask and we should ask of God.

God's Decision Is Best   Shari, a young friend of mine, desperately wanted a part in a movie that was being shot in her city. She prayed about being chosen as a part of the local cast, and she asked others to join with her in prayer. When the day came for auditions, Shari wasn't chosen. She was heartbroken. Frankly, she didn't understand why God had said no to something that she wanted so much and for which she showed so much talent. She was excluded from several social outings as her friends began to form new associations with the "movie people."

As the months passed, Shari began to hear reports about the behavior of her friends who had been chosen for the movie. They were becoming quite rebellious at home and at school. They began experimenting with drugs during the course of the filming, and they began to drink excessively. Shari watched silently as her friends became rowdier and, eventually, even began to break the law.

After about six months, the day came when Shari said to her mother, "I'm glad I wasn't chosen to be in the movie. I'm afraid I might not have been strong enough to withstand the pressure to go along with the rest of the gang. I could be in serious trouble by now."

Shari realized that even though she had experienced hurt initially at God's saying no, God had actually spared her a far greater hurt that could have impacted her entire life.

13 • Sometimes God Says "Not Now"

To everything there is a season,
A time for every purpose under heaven.
—Ecclesiastes 3:1

The Bible has a great deal to say about the "fullness of time," the precise, appropriate moment, from God's perspective, when things should happen for maximum and eternal good. How important it is that we teach our children about the *fullness* of God's time for certain things in their lives. And how difficult it is for children, sometimes, to comprehend that lesson.

One of the best ways I know to convey the concept of "God's perfect timing" is to plant seeds with your child. I suggest you choose beans as a plant to grow since they tend to germinate and produce quickly. Pray with your child as you plant your seeds,

Heavenly Father, we ask you to give us beans.

As the seed comes up, pray again,

Heavenly Father, we ask you to give us beans.

As the leaves began to form and the plant grows tall, pray yet again,

Heavenly Father, we ask you to give us beans.

The day will come when the pods begin to form.

Heavenly Father, we ask you to give us beans.

Finally, the pods will be ready to pick and to open—revealing beans!

Point out to your child that God had *begun* to answer your prayer for beans at the time you first planted the seed. The fullness of the answer, however, was actually realized at the moment when you opened the pod to find beans.

Teach your child that many of our prayers are like that prayer for beans. They are good and right petitions before the throne of God, but we are often praying in advance of God's right moment for answering our prayer fully. What shall we do when God's answer is "not yet" or "not now"? It is at those times that we need to *keep* praying and believing.

Our son Rob had no doubt whatsoever that he would pass his driving test on his sixteenth birthday. He had an ardent interest in hot rods and motorcycles and had quickly mastered the basic skills of driving. He failed, however, to pass the test on his first attempt. Embarrassed and hurt, Rob realized that God had said, "Not now." A few months later, Rob passed the test and with a near-perfect score. However, that experience cooled his interest in cars and cycles. Simultaneously, his love for the Lord began to grow by leaps and bounds, and he developed a new interest—medicine. Today, Rob is a physician and an assistant professor at a medical school where he is actively involved in cancer research and bone marrow transplants. Sometimes God says "not now" in order to divert our attention to His higher purposes for our lives.

In nearly all cases, "not now" answers teach us patience, and as we continue to pray and believe, our faith grows, too.

14 • Pray Before a Visit to the Doctor, Dentist, or Hospital

You will keep him in perfect peace,
Whose mind is stayed on You,
Because he trusts in You.
—Isaiah 26:3

Is your child fearful of a visit to the doctor or dentist? Pray about that appointment with your child.

Children generally have two fears in this area. The first is that of pain or discomfort. Teach your child to ask for help from the Lord.

> *Help me to be able to stand any pain that may come. Help me to trust You to be able to endure any procedure and to know that any hurt I feel is only going to last a little while. If I need to have a shot, help the nurse to give it to me in the right way so that it won't hurt very much. Help me to be brave. Help me to trust You for my complete healing.*

The second fear is that of the unknown. Perhaps more than any other environment your child experiences, a doctor's or dentist's office is filled with equipment that looks ominous, surfaces that seem cold and hard, and procedures that are foreign. Teach your child to call on the name of the Lord when he feels fear:

Jesus be with me. Jesus help me. Jesus, take away any fear or worry that might try to take over my mind and my heart. Help me to trust You to bring me through this experience victoriously.

Our son Rob faced surgery for torn ligaments when he was a child. As he was wheeled away from us into the surgical theatre, we saw his face turn ashen and terror fill his eyes. The surgeon came to us a few minutes later and said that Rob's blood pressure had soared to a dangerous level.

We asked to speak with Rob briefly. We said, "Honey, just call on the name of the Lord. Call out to Jesus. He'll be with you in this." We heard Rob begin to say, "Jesus . . . Jesus . . . Jesus." He continued to repeat only the name of the Lord, over and over and over. Within a few minutes, a calm came over his entire being, his blood pressure dropped, and he went through the surgery without any further incident.

In times of fear, your child may not be able to think of a prayer. He may not be able to form words or even to think of words. Panic can erase all logic, all language ability, all muscle coordination. Teach your child to say only one word as a prayer: the name of Jesus.

15 • Pray Before the Big Event

Blessed be the Lord,
Because He has heard the voice of my
*   supplications!*
The Lord is my strength and my shield;
My heart trusted in Him, and I am helped;
Therefore my heart greatly rejoices,
And with my song I will praise Him.
                    —Psalm 28:6–7

Encourage your child to pray each and every time he faces a challenge to his skill, ability, talent, or witness:

* before the big game;
* before the recital;
* before the on-stage debut;
* before the court hearing;
* before the concert.

Before any experience in which your child has a doubt as to his own ability to do his best. Teach your child Philippians 4:13. "I can do all things through Christ who strengthens me." Encourage your child to make that a prayer,

> *Heavenly Father, I trust Your word to me that I can,*
> *I can do all things through Christ who strengthens*
> *me.*

About what specifically can your child pray with confidence?

• For the ability to do his best.

> *Lord, You are the One who created me and You are the One who has given me talents and abilities. Help me to do my best so that I might be a good witness for You.*

Pray, too, that every other person involved will also give a peak performance.

> *Help each one to do his best, that we might play well together as a team.*

• For the ability to remember all the plays, all the notes, all the calls, all the steps, all the facts, all the Scriptures that pertain to the moment.

> *Lord, I trust You to cause my mind to work the way You created it to work. Help me to think clearly and to be sharp mentally.*

• For safety.

> *Lord, help us to do this without injury or harm to any person.*

In some cases, the potential injury may be emotional.

Help us, Lord, not to embarrass any person or to cause anyone to become hurt emotionally. Protect me, Lord, from doing anything that might cause lasting hurt to my heart.

- For confidence.

Help me, Lord, to overcome my jitters. Don't let me be overcome by nervousness. Let me see this as an opportunity to bring glory to You and to bless others.

- For graciousness in winning or losing.

Help us, Lord, to be good sports whether we win or lose. Help us to show your compassion and loving-kindness to those who have competed against us.

Encourage your child to see that every experience in life is like a thread that the Lord is weaving together into a wonderful piece of fabric. The wins are like the warp; the losses are like the woof. It takes both warp and woof—threads running both ways—to make a strong piece of cloth.

16 • Pray for the Desire to Obey

Remind them to be subject to rulers and authorities, to obey, to be ready for every good work, to speak evil of no one, to be peaceable, gentle, showing humility to all men.

—Titus 3:1–2

Obedience is one of the most important lessons any child ever learns—and one of the toughest. All temptation converges on obedience, doesn't it? We are tempted to disobey what we know to be right in God's eyes.

Encourage your child to pray that the Lord will give him or her a desire to obey, and specifically to obey you as a parent or adult with authority over the child.

> *Lord, help me to* want *to obey my parents when they tell me to do my homework.*

> *Help me, heavenly Father, to* want *to avoid the people, places, and things that my parents say are bad for me.*

> *I ask you, Lord Jesus, to help me* want *to do what is pleasing to You.*

Is your teenager beginning to show signs of rebellion? Pray with him or her about it. I did this with our son when he was about thirteen years old.

Ask Your Child to Pray for You One night, after a rebellious scene, I confronted my son and heard myself saying, "Please pray for me. I want to be a good mother to you. That's my responsibility before God, to train you up to love and serve Him.

"I know you didn't choose me to be your mother. God chose me for that job. God chose you to be my son and to put us together as a family. Would you pray that God will give me wisdom about what I should say to you and how I should train you? Please ask God to help me. I don't want to aggravate you. I want to do things that will eventually bring you blessing."

Something happened that night. The spirit of rebellion in my son began to dissipate. What deep assurance I felt when, through our tears, my son prayed for me and for his obedience.

Finally, pray for and with your child that your child will always be obedient to what the Lord calls him to do, whether he wants to do it or not. Read the story of young Samuel to your child (1 Sam. 3:1–10). Read the parable of Jesus about cheerful obedience in Matthew 21:28–31. Pray with your child,

Heavenly Father, help me always to say yes when you call and to respond cheerfully and willingly to anything that You ask me to do.

17 • Pray for the Ability to Think Clearly and to Learn

Let this mind be in you which was also in Christ Jesus.

—Philippians 2:5

Paul wrote to his coworker Timothy about the nature we are to have in Christ Jesus. He said, "God has not given us a spirit of fear, but of power and of love and of a sound mind" (2 Tim. 1:7). Luke described the young boy Jesus as increasing in "wisdom and stature, and in favor with God and men" (Luke 2:52).

The goal we must hold out to our children is that they develop a sound mind, one that is able to discern clearly the difference between good and evil and one that is firmly established in the things of God. We must always point our children toward the acquisition of wisdom, the ability to think and reason in any situation the way that Jesus would think and reason.

Toward this end, we can encourage our children to pray, "Cause my mind to think the way You made it, Lord!" Specifically, your child can pray for *the ability to concentrate.*

Help me, heavenly Father, to be able to shut off everything else but this one topic. Help me to focus all of my attention on learning this material.

Your child can also pray for the ability to reason things through.

Help me, heavenly Father, to see this issue from Your perspective. Guide my thoughts, Lord, and don't let me go astray in my thinking.

Teach your child that his mind is a gift from, and a creation of, God and that God intends for us to use our minds to think good thoughts and to solve problems so this world can be a better place for all people to live. Teach your child Philippians 4:8. Turn that verse into a prayer,

Help me, Heavenly Father, to see your truth in this subject matter. Help me to see the noble thing in this history lesson, to focus on the lovely aspects of this story, to look for the good report in this science lesson.

Finally, encourage your child to pray before starting any new unit of study, lesson, test, or homework assignment:

Help me to learn this to the best of my ability, to understand this material and to be able to see how I

might use it some day. Help me to ask questions when I don't understand. Give my teachers wisdom in teaching this lesson and help them to have patience with me as I learn. Thank you for giving me the opportunity to learn more about Your creation and the principles that You have established for my life.

18 • Pray for the Ability to Know

It is the Spirit who bears witness, because the Spirit is truth.

—1 John 5:6

The Spirit of God cannot lie. He only reveals truth. Encourage your child to ask for truth from the Holy Spirit, that he might have the ability to know what is good, right, and true before God. Ask your child to pray,

> *Heavenly Father, show me what is good. Help me to create good things by your Holy Spirit.*

As your child embarks on a creative project, such as a story, a painting, a musical composition, teach him to pray,

> *Help me, heavenly Father, to produce something that reflects the beauty and harmony and goodness of Your creation.*

Your child faces many decisions every day in his relationships with his peers. This is an excellent prayer for your child to say when he is feeling peer pressure.

> *Heavenly Father, show me what is right in Your eyes. Help me to discern good from evil, right from wrong. Give me boldness to stand up for what You show me is right.*

Is your child struggling with his own emotions—his own desires, his own anger or resentments or bitterness, his own loneliness? Encourage your child to pray that the Lord might show Him the truth about who He is in Christ Jesus.

> *Heavenly Father, show me what You see when you see me. Reveal to me that my sins have been blotted out when I ask You for forgiveness. Let me feel Your presence when I am lonely. Give me the desire to forgive others so that I might be made more like Jesus every day.*

Encourage your child to pray for the ability to remember what he learns that is good, right, and true.

> *Heavenly Father, help me to remember this lesson always.*

When King Jehoshaphat of Israel found himself and his people surrounded by three fierce enemy tribes, he cried out to the Lord in prayer. His prayer is one that every child can and should learn:

We have no power against this great multitude that is coming against us; nor do we know what to do, but our eyes are upon You (2 Chron. 20:12).

What should your child do when he doesn't know what to do? Pray—and ask God for His answer!

19 • Pray for Our Nation's Leaders

Therefore I exhort first of all that supplications, prayers, intercessions, and giving of thanks be made for all men, for kings and all who are in authority, that we may lead a quiet and peaceable life in all godliness and reverence.
—1 Timothy 2:1–2

The Bible states clearly in a number of places that we are to respect those in authority. For example, Exodus 22:28 says that we "shall not revile God, nor curse a ruler of [our] people." The Word of God also teaches us that all authority ultimately comes from God, that He raises up whom He will into positions of power, and that He puts down other leaders according to His divine purposes (Ps. 22:8, Prov. 8:15–16, Daniel 2:20–21.)

Encourage your child to pray for our nation's leaders in a fivefold way:

1. Pray for their salvation.

Heavenly Father, I pray that the leaders of our nation will come to have a deep spiritual relationship with You and that they will learn to hear Your voice as they make important decisions about our nation.

2. Pray that our leaders will make wise decisions.

Heavenly Father, please fill [name] with Your wisdom. Cause him or her to make decisions that are pleasing to You and according to Your divine plan.

3. Pray for the physical and emotional strength of our leaders, and that they might have good health.

Heavenly Father, please keep [name] well and strong physically, mentally, and emotionally. Keep him or her safe and healthy!

4. Pray for the families of our leaders. The stress and strain of leadership takes its toll on the families of a leader.

Heavenly Father, please be with the families of [name]. Keep them well and strong, safe and healthy, and their relationships loving and faithful.

5. We are to pray that the leaders will establish an atmosphere whereby the people of our nation will want to know and follow a "knowledge of the truth."

Heavenly Father, help [names] to live a life that is a good example to the people of our land. Help them to lead us in finding Your answers to the problems that we face. We pray they will make and enforce good laws that are fair to all of the people.

The National Children's Prayer Network* in Washington, D.C. is organized to assist children in Sunday schools and Christian schools across the nation to pray daily for our lawmakers. The children write letters to our nation's leaders to let them know that they are praying for them. You can do this, too.

Praying for the leaders of our nation develops in children an understanding of the responsibility of leadership and challenges them to take their place as they grow to maturity.

---

* To contact the National Children's Prayer Network, you may write Lin Story, P.O. Box 9683, Washington, D.C. 20016.

20 • Pray for the Nations

His name shall endure forever;
His name shall continue as long as the
sun.
And men shall be blessed in Him;
All nations shall call Him blessed.
—Psalm 72:17

As Christians, we acknowledge the Lord as our King. He is "high above all nations" (Ps. 113:4) and "King forever" (Ps. 10:16). He is the King of glory, the Lord strong and mighty (Ps. 24:8). He is the King of kings and the Lord of lords (Rev. 17:14).

God has a world view. We should have one, too. God is vitally concerned about all people in all nations. We should be, too.

Do you have a globe, world map, or an atlas in your home? Use it as a focal point for prayer times with your children. Choose one nation and concentrate your prayer time on it.

- *Pray for the leaders of the nation,* that they might come to know the Lord and that they make decisions that reflect God's wisdom.

    Heavenly Father, help the leaders of this nation to rule in a way that brings honor to Your name.

• *Pray for the Christians in the nation.* Are they being persecuted? Pray for their safety. Pray that the Holy Spirit will bring revival among them and that they will win many of their friends and neighbors to the Lord.

> *Heavenly Father, be with my brothers and sisters in Christ who are living in this land. Light a fire in their souls that they might be quick to share the Good News of Your Son, Jesus Christ.*

• *Pray for the children in the nation.* Do they have sufficient food and clothing? Is there a war raging in their land? Pray for specific needs. Pray that the children will come to hear about Jesus and to love Him as their Savior and Lord.

> *Heavenly Father, take care of the little children in this land. Give them food and water and warmth and friends and a safe place to sleep. Send someone to them to tell them about Jesus.*

• *Pray for the missionaries and church leaders at work in that nation.* Pray that the Lord will protect them and give them great courage in proclaiming His Word.

> *Heavenly Father, help the pastors and evangelists in this nation to show love to the people and to teach them about Jesus. Keep them safe and well. Give them courage and boldness.*

Praying in this manner helps your child to develop an "outward view," a view toward

- evangelism;
- reaching out to others and caring about them no matter their race, color, or culture;
- developing a concern that the practical needs of suffering people be met;
- binding their hearts with fellow Christians around the world.

The Scriptures ask us to pray for the blessing of Israel (Gen. 12:3) and for the peace of Jerusalem (Ps. 11:6–7).

Pray for Jesus to come and rule the world in true peace from Jerusalem as He promises.

In and through prayer, help your child see the world as the Father sees it, as the home of *all* His beloved children.

21 • Pray About Events and News Stories That Touch Your Heart

> *In all things [Jesus] had to be made like His brethren, that He might be a merciful and faithful High Priest in things pertaining to God . . . for in that He Himself has suffered, being tempted, He is able to aid those who are tempted.*
>
> —Hebrews 2:17–18

Turn times of concern into times of prayer.

- Is your child concerned about a story he has heard on a television newscast?
- Have you witnessed an accident on the freeway?
- Has a tragedy of some type occurred at your child's school?
- Does your child ask questions about the faces of the children he sees on the milk carton?

Establish a pattern for your child of taking *all* needs of others to the Lord in prayer. The needs may be remote or close to home, big or little. They may be physical, spiritual, material, or emotional in nature.

Perhaps your child has just heard a radio or television report of a major earthquake in a faraway place. He is concerned about it. Channel his concern for others into prayer for them.

> *Heavenly Father, please be with the people who have lost their homes and their loved ones. Comfort their hearts. Give them strength to get through this difficult time. Provide a safe place for them to go. Help them not to be afraid.*

Lindy and Jill, acquaintances of mine, recently asked their mother if they could pray for the missing children whose faces appear on the milk cartons they use every morning as they eat their cereal. They now include their names in their breakfast mealtime prayer:

> *Heavenly Father, help these children* (whom they list by name) *to be found so they can go home to their mothers and fathers. Keep them safe and comfort the hearts of their parents.*

If your child expresses concern after hearing a report about a terrorist bombing, ask your child what Jesus would do. "I think he would heal the people who got hurt and that He'd make sure the people who did this were caught so they couldn't do it again." Pray along those lines.

> *Heavenly Father, please heal the people who have been injured. Take away the fear in their minds and heal the wounds of their bodies. We ask that You help the police capture the people who set off this bomb.*

Encouraging your child to pray as she hears or sees news events that trouble her takes your child's focus off herself and her own fear. It also turns your child's aimless feelings of helplessness into a productive expression that points toward God and toward healing and wholeness.

22 • Pray for the Needy People in Your City

When he flees to one of those cities, and stands at the entrance of the gate of the city, and declares his case in the hearing of the elders of that city, they shall take him into the city as one of them, and give him a place, that he may dwell among them.

—Joshua 20:4

Nearly every child in our nation today will, at some time, encounter a destitute person, someone living in despair. It may be a person or family that comes to your church to receive a meal or a sack of groceries. It may be a person or group of people your child sees as you walk or drive the streets of your city. It may be a report your child sees on television.

Very few thoughts are scarier to a child than the thought that he might not have a home—a bed to call his own, a closet in which to hang his clothes, a place to play and feel safe from the world. What can your child do in confronting his own fears and in expressing concern for the homeless? He can pray!

Homeless people aren't the only people who live in a state of despair. Many people who have homes and jobs still can barely make ends meet financially. Their life is a daily struggle for minimal levels of food, shelter, and clothing. Other families face serious, terminal, or protracted health problems.

When your child encounters a needy person, encourage your child to pray,

> *Heavenly Father, keep this person safe tonight. Give him a secure place to sleep and people around him who will speak a kind word.*

Encourage your child to pray,

> *Heavenly Father, help my friend who is going through this illness. Ease the suffering. Take away the pain. Heal my friend's body. Don't let my friend become discouraged or depressed. Give my friend Your joy and comfort his family.*

Praying for others who are in need helps children develop an unselfish and compassionate attitude. It keeps pride from their hearts and causes them to be more sensitive to those who are in trouble.

23 • Pray for Friends and Neighbors "To Be in Heaven with Us"

For God so loved the world that He gave His only begotten Son, that whoever believes in Him should not perish but have everlasting life.

—John 3:16

Help your child develop a deep compassion for the eternal souls of others. Join your child in praying that your child's friends will come to have a personal relationship with the Lord Jesus.

When our daughter LeeAnn was in second grade, she said to me one day after she came home from school, "My friend Linda needs to come home with me after school tomorrow."

"Well, LeeAnn," I reminded her, "that's just not going to be possible. We already have other plans." On the verge of tears she responded, "You don't understand, mother, she's *got* to come over *tomorrow.*"

"Why?" I asked. "Why can't she come later in the week?"

"Because she wants to invite Jesus into her heart, and you have to help her do that. She doesn't want to wait any longer."

LeeAnn was right—those other plans could wait! Linda came over the next afternoon and the three of us prayed together that she would have a personal relationship with the Lord Jesus.

Encourage your child to pray,

> *Heavenly Father, help my friends to come to know You and to love You before they die so we can live together in heaven with You and each other forever.*

Let your child know that it's OK for him to pray with his friends.

> *Heavenly Father, my friend wants to know You like I do. I ask You to forgive my friend for his sins and to give him a clean heart. I ask You to send the Holy Spirit to live inside him and to help him to live in a way that is pleasing to you. Help my friend to love You every day of his life, to talk to You often, and to read the Bible so he can learn more about You. I ask You to do this in the name of Jesus.*

When your child prays for the eternal soul of a friend, she develops a compassion for that friend. She learns what it means to love another person as a spiritual "brother" or "sister."

24 • Pray for the Pastor, Sunday School Teacher, and Other Church Leaders

I would not stretch out my hand against the Lord's anointed. And indeed, as your life was valued much this day in my eyes, so let my life be valued much in the eyes of the Lord, and let Him deliver me out of all tribulation.

—1 Samuel 26:23–24

Tell your child the story about Moses, Aaron, and Hur as the Israelites fought against Amalek (Exod. 17:10–13).

As long as Moses held up his hand, Israel prevailed in the battle. When he let down his hand, the enemy Amalek began to win. The Bible says that Moses' hands became "heavy" and he could no longer hold them up. Aaron and Hur "supported his hands, one on one side, and the other on the other side; and his hands were steady until the going down of the sun" (Exod. 17:12). The Israelites won the battle that day.

As a part of the church, your child can help "lift up the hands" of those in leadership by praying for them.

• Pray that they will continue to be strong and well in body, mind, and spirit.

> *Heavenly Father, keep my pastor and my Sunday school teacher and all those who lead our church in good health. Keep them strong and well in every area of their lives.*

• Pray that they will experience the joy of the Lord every day.

> *Heavenly Father, fill my pastor and my Sunday school teacher with Your presence and give them joy in their hearts. Help them to see that their work is important and that they are going to be rewarded by You for all of the good work that they do.*

• Pray that they will grow in their ability to teach and to lead.

> *Heavenly Father, help my pastor and my Sunday school teacher understand Your Word more every day. Help them to teach us Your Word so that we can understand it, too. Help my pastor follow Your leading and make right decisions for the church.*

- Pray that they will have a growing love for all of the people in the church.

  Heavenly Father, help my pastor and Sunday school teacher be kind to every person in our church, to treat everybody with fairness and love, and to be patient with all of us children.

- Pray they will be true to the Word of the Lord always.

  Heavenly Father, keep my pastor and Sunday school teacher from falling into any kind of error or sin. Give them the courage not only to know Your will, but to do it every day of their lives.

Your child's relationship with those in spiritual leadership positions is an important one. Let the relationship be bathed in prayer.

25 • Pray for Family Members

Confess your trespasses to one another, and pray for one another, that you may be healed. The effective, fervent prayer of a righteous man avails much.

—James 5:16

Encourage your child to pray for you, your spouse, his brothers and sisters, and other relatives and family friends. Call them by name. Remember them and their needs before the Lord.

You may want to have a family prayer list that you consult regularly, perhaps keeping it in your family Bible and referring to it for a time of prayer as part of your daily Bible-reading schedule.

Encourage your child to pray for:

• Health and safety.

> *Heavenly Father, I ask You to keep each member of my family strong and well. Keep them from accidents and any kind of harm.*

• Parents to love each other.

Heavenly Father, I ask You to help my mother and daddy love each other, to be kind to one another, and to help each other in every way they can.

• Parents to know what's right to do.

Heavenly Father, I ask You to help my mother and daddy to do what is right for me. Help them to be patient with me and to make good decisions about my life. Help them to understand me and to show their love for me in ways that I can receive it.

• For problems the family member is facing.

Heavenly Father, help my loved one. Show him Your solution for this problem, Your way out of this diffi-culty, Your provision for this need.

Ask your child to pray for you when you are sick, discouraged about something, facing a problem. Receive your child's prayers! Thank your child for praying for you. When you are well again or the problem has been resolved, let your child know that his prayers have been answered. Praise God together for answered prayer.

• Have your children been fighting all morning? Call them together for a time of prayer. Ask them to pray one for the other.

- Has it been one of those days when all of the family members seemed to be running in circles? Call the family together for prayer. Let every person voice his petition to Father God.
- Has it been a week when nothing in your family life seemed to go according to your plans? Pray together as a family. Give each child an opportunity to pray.

26 • Pray for Teachers and the School Principal

So teach us . . . that we may gain a heart for wisdom.

—Psalm 90:12

Encourage your child to pray frequently for his teachers and those in leadership positions at his school—the principal, the dean, the coach, and so forth. Have your child pray that those who teach him will have:

- Wisdom in teaching. Teaching requires more than knowledge; it requires an ability to convey that knowledge so that it is received, understood, applied, and valued.

    Heavenly Father, please give my teacher Your wisdom. Let my teacher see clearly what it is that is most important for me to know. Help her to know how to keep discipline in the classroom.

- An ability to communicate.

    Heavenly Father, help my teacher to explain things

thoroughly and to give clear instructions. Help me to understand what my teacher says.

• Fairness.

Heavenly Father, help my teacher treat us all fairly. Don't let my teacher have special "pets." Help my teacher give us each an opportunity to do our best.

• Patience.

Heavenly Father, help my teacher to be patient with me and with all of the children in my class. Give her a good sense of humor, Lord. Help her to be gentle in her discipline.

• A soft heart for God.

Heavenly Father, help my teacher to grow in his relationship with You. Keep his heart tender toward Your Spirit and toward Your leading. Don't let him criticize the things of God or the people of God.

Has your child disobeyed a teacher and been punished for it? Encourage your child to pray for forgiveness and a restoration of his relationship with the teacher.

Heavenly Father, I'm sorry for what I did at school today. Please forgive me. Help my teacher not to hold this against me in the future. Please heal my relationship with my teacher.

Make certain that your child's prayers for his or her teacher, and others in positions of school leadership, are kept positive and uplifting. Join your child in these prayers. Send a message to your child that you, the teacher, and the child are a team that is working together for your child's good.

27 • Pray Any Time and Anywhere

Help me, O Lord my God!
Oh, save me according to Your mercy,
That they may know that this is Your
hand—
That You, LORD, have done it!
—Psalm 109:26–27

Let your child know that it is 100 percent permissible to pray any time and anywhere. He can pray:

- alone or with others;
- softly to himself or aloud;
- long or short.
- No matter what!

Let your child know that he doesn't need to postpone his prayers until the next visit to church, or even wait until the family prayer time before he goes to bed. He can pray at the time a need occurs. God has an open-door policy night and day.

Assure your child that any place on the earth can become a prayer room.

- Daniel prayed in a den filled with hungry lions.
- Shadrach, Meshach, and Abed-Nego prayed in a burning, fiery furnace, even as an angry king and people watched.

- Peter cried out in prayer as he began to sink after walking on the waters of the Sea of Galilee, with all of the other disciples watching from the boat.
- Paul and Silas prayed and sang praises in a jail cell.

Our daughter LeeAnn turned the corral of a Montana ranch into a prayer room one afternoon as she was taming an appaloosa horse. We came to the corral railings to hear her calling out to the Lord for help and safety, completely oblivious to any around her.

Assure your child that our Father God always hears your child's prayer and will act on her behalf. That's what Jesus showed us when He stopped on a trip through Jericho to heal a blind man named Bartimaeus, when He stopped on His way to Jairus's house to heal a woman who reached out to touch the hem of His garment, when He interrupted His own sermon to heal a man with a withered hand, and when he postponed a prayer retreat to talk to little children.

Let your child know that prayer is a time of direct communication between your child and God.

28 • Pray in Times of Personal Emergency

Save now, I pray, O Lord.
—Psalm 118:25

Prayers do not need to be flowery, long, or stated grammatically to be heard, understood, and acted upon by Father God. Assure your child of that fact. God hears SOS prayers. The Scriptures are filled with examples:

- Jonah, in the belly of a great fish;
- Paul, in a storm at sea;
- Esther, as she faced a death sentence along with her people.

God hears and answers our cries for help.

When I was a child, I was riding my bicycle one day when I was confronted by a large, mean, and very fast-running dog. At least, that is the way I remember that dog. The more I tried to talk reasonably to the dog, the louder it barked. The faster I pedaled my bicycle, the faster it ran, nipping at my heels on the pedals. Finally, I called out to God in desperation, "Lord, I need help *now!*" Immediately, the dog stopped in his tracks, ceased barking, and when I finally turned around to see what had happened, he was calmly walking back home.

"Lord, I need help *now"* is a simple prayer that any child can learn, even at a very young age. The prayer actually has four important lessons in it for your child.

- *Lord.* Your child is calling on the Lord for help, not upon any other person, organization, or thing. The Lord should always be your child's first line of thought in times of trouble or emergency.
- *I need.* It is important for your child to recognize his dependency upon the Lord, and the fact that he has needs that only the Lord can meet. Nobody is completely self-sufficient. Acknowledging need is an important step for your child to take in his spiritual growth.
- *Help.* The Lord's help comes in many different forms. Sometimes it's a deliverance from a mean dog. Sometimes it's deliverance from mean people. Sometimes it's deliverance from circumstances, sickness, the threat of death, an impending accident. Sometimes it's deliverance from the influence of evil powers. The Lord's ability to help is not limited. It is available around the clock.
- *Now.* The Lord God is always in the "now" moments of our lives. He is not slow to act or reluctant to act. Very often a child's prayers for "now" help are answered with immediacy.

This prayer is ultimately a prayer of utter dependence upon the Lord to do what only He can do in our lives—deliver us from evil.

29 • Pray That God Will Change Things

We know that all things work together for good to those who love God, to those who are the called according to His purpose.

—Romans 8:28

Our privilege as sons and daughters of God—no matter our physical ages—is to ask God to deliver us from any form of evil and to cause circumstances to change for our good.

We experienced this in a powerful way when our children were young teenagers. New neighbors moved in across the street from us, and shortly thereafter problems began to surface, mostly involving their two older teenage sons. The neighbor boys freely consumed alcohol and used drugs as they worked on their cars in the driveway. The more we tried to befriend the family, the worse the problems seemed to grow.

The boys played loud music from midafternoon until late at night and all weekend long. One day as I was gardening with the children, we noticed that the earth was shaking under our knees from the vibrations of the music being played down the hill and across the street. We began to pray there in the yard.

Heavenly Father, we feel as if we are living under the influence of evil, and we ask you to deliver us from it. We ask you to deliver these teenage boys across the street from sin and to bring them into a salvation experience with You or to remove them from this neighborhood. Thank you, Lord Jesus, for being our Deliverer.

The children also prayed,

Heavenly Father, we ask that the family that comes to live in this house would be a Christian family. Please, Lord, send a family with a boy and a girl so we can have Christian playmates.

The Lord answered the prayers exactly. Two months later, the family was transferred to another city. A lovely Christian family moved into the house within a few days, and they had a son and a daughter for our children to play with.

Encourage your child to pray for deliverance from evil and for the establishment of good.

- It may be a prayer that another child at school will stop his bullying, or her arguing, or his pestering, or her teasing.
- It may be a prayer that pornographic materials will be removed from a neighborhood quick-stop store.
- It may be a prayer that a mean or noisome animal in

the neighborhood will be given a new home (away from yours).

At some point in your child's life, he or she will undoubtedly be confronted by evil. Arm your child in advance with three prayers: one for deliverance, another for God's best provision, and one for the courage to run away from evil.

30 • Thank God for Good Things When They Come

Thanks be to God for His indescribable gift!
—2 Corinthians 9:15

Every perfect gift in our lives ultimately comes from God, our loving Provider:

- each day of your child's life and every hour in it;
- each meal;
- each breath he takes, each beat of his heart;
- each word of encouragement, hug, or kiss from a loving parent;
- each toy or gift item she receives;
- each opportunity and challenge to grow;
- each bit of information, insight, and revelation;
- each friend and loved one;
- *everything!*

Encourage your child to honor God as the Source of all good things in his life and to honor God as the supreme Gift-giver. Encourage your child to offer a prayer of thanks any time she experiences something good.

Four-year-old Catherine prayed this bedtime prayer as she lay in her aunt's king-sized bed one evening during an overnight stay: "Thank you, Lord, that we got to eat pizza tonight. Thank you, Lord, that I get to spend the night with my aunt and sleep in this big bed." She said with great gusto, "And *thank you,* God, that I get to eat cereal for breakfast!"

No item is too small to be worthy of thanks. No gift is too small. No treat is too trivial.

Our two-year-old grandson Joshua is a living bundle of enthusiasm. Nothing seems too small for his exuberant acknowledgement. This past Christmas he came to me after we had all exchanged presents and said with great excitement, "Aren't you *glad* you got that present?" I sense a great future ahead for him as a child of praise!

Encourage your child to memorize James 1:17. "Every good gift and every perfect gift is from above, and comes down from the Father of lights, with whom there is no variation or shadow of turning."

• Prayers of thanksgiving focus the attention of your child on what he has, not on what he doesn't have.

• Prayers of thanksgiving help your child develop a grateful heart.

• Prayers of thanksgiving turn your child's attention to God as the Giver behind every gift, and lessens his reliance on people for those things that bring true joy into our lives.

31 • Praise God for the Things He Has Made

In the beginning God created the heavens and the earth.

—Genesis 1:1

Acknowledge God as the Creator of all things! Teach your child to praise Him for His creation:

- For stars that fill the sky and the moon that glows so brilliantly, changing its shape by degrees each night.
- For bubbling streams and mighty ocean waves and wispy waterfalls and clear mountain lakes.
- For cool sand and polished rocks and shells that wash up on the seashore.
- For the animals of the forest, jungle, and desert. For the animals in your neighborhood. For your child's pet.
- For nutritious food and clean water to drink.

All of nature is a living panorama of God's goodness. Take a nature walk with your child and turn it into a praise service. Let your child offer praise for each item he sees:

Praise God for the caterpillar. Praise God for the leaf. Praise God for the tree. Thank you, God, for making these things. They give me pleasure. They teach me lessons. Thank you for the gift they are to me!

Praising God for His creation helps to establish two principles in your child's life. First, God is the Creator. Every aspect of His creation is "original" and "special." What God has created, He knows how to sustain, mend, heal, and cause to grow and multiply.

All life-giving acts and manifestations of creativity ultimately come from God. Teach your child to praise Him,

I thank You and praise You, O God, for all of Your handiwork. Thank You for making me. Thank You for taking care of me and for making me a one-of-a-kind original.

Second, God has a purpose for every aspect of His creation, including the life of your child. Teach your child to praise Him,

I thank You and praise You, O God, for the way in which You have created me. Thank You for the talents, abilities, skills, and opportunities You have given me. Cause me to bloom where You have planted me.

32 • Tell God Exactly How You Feel

I am weary with my groaning;
All night I make my bed swim;
I drench my couch with my tears.
My eye wastes away because of grief;
It grows old because of all my enemies.
—Psalm 6:6–7

Give your child the assurance that God is never going to be shocked or surprised by what your child says to Him. Let your child know that he can be totally honest with God and express anything that is on his heart.

Your child can tell God when he is

- **Wondering about life.** God delights in hearing your child's questions. He will find a way to answer them. A little friend of mine was once overheard asking the Lord in prayer,

   And God, I've been wondering—do caterpillars like cottage cheese?

- **Troubled or concerned.** Children are capable of worry. Children can get ulcers, too. Through prayer, your child experiences the peace of God.

Help me not to be afraid, God, of what the future holds. Fill my heart with Your peace.

- **Angry.** Better to pray than to pout! Anger dissipates as your child prays and trusts the situation to God.

  I'm angry and upset about this, God. Free me from this feeling of anger as I trust You to take care of this situation.

- **Happy.** God wants to know how happy your child is when he wins a victory, or receives a nice compliment, or does well at something he's attempted. God delights in your child's successes as much as you do as a parent.

  Heavenly Father, thank you for the good thing that happened to me today. I know You planned it just for me!

- **Sad.** Does your child carry a deep burden of sorrow? Has she been rejected? Is she discouraged at repeated failures? Encourage her to turn to the Lord in prayer and to express just how she feels to the Lord.

  Heavenly Father, this situation makes me so sad I just want to cry all the time. Please bind up my broken heart and take away this ache that I feel. Show me things I can do to make this situation better.

Teach your child that she can trust God with things that she wouldn't even tell her best friend. God can and will keep your child's secret, He can and will forgive any sin your child confesses to Him, He can and will act on your child's behalf.

Prayer about feelings helps your child develop a truly "conversational" relationship with the Lord. Your child will come to know what it means to "walk with Him, and talk with Him" on a daily basis.

33 ● Pray for the Ability to Forgive Others (Who Hurt You Unintentionally)

Whenever you stand praying, if you have anything against anyone, forgive him, that your Father in heaven may also forgive you your trespasses. But if you do not forgive, neither will your Father in heaven forgive your trespasses.

—Mark 11:25

Children are beginners when it comes to interpreting human behavior and the actions of others. We adults sometimes forget that fact. Children often take the words and actions of others far more personally or more deeply than is intended by the other party.

Prayer helps to heal the injured emotions and feelings of rejection that children feel when they are unintentionally excluded from games or parties, overlooked by teachers, punished unfairly, left out of a secret, or ignored by someone with whom they would like to be friends.

● Encourage your child to pray,

Heavenly Father, hold my heart in Your hand so that no matter what others may do to me, I will feel Your warmth of security, and love.

- Encourage your child to admit how he feels in prayer and to ask the Lord to resolve any negative feelings he harbors toward others.

Heavenly Father, my feelings were hurt today by what my friend said. Help me not to feel so bad. Help me to forgive my friend in my heart.

- Encourage your child to ask God to give him an understanding of why other people act the way they do.

Heavenly Father, help me to understand why my friend did what she did. Help me to see my friend as You do. Help me to love her and to be patient with her.

- Encourage your child to ask for restraint not to strike back.

Heavenly Father, help me to forget what happened and to get over this desire I have to strike back and get even.

When your child forgives others he opens up the

door to receive forgiveness in his own life. Forgiving others is the key to a life uncluttered by bitterness and resentment, which develop into meanness. Encourage your child to forgive freely!

34 ● Pray for Those Who Persecute You (Intentionally)

Love your enemies, bless those who curse you, do good to those who hate you, and pray for those who spitefully use you and persecute you, that you may be sons of your Father in heaven.

—Matthew 5:44–45

Persecution is intentional. It is often premeditated. It may come because your child is standing up for what is right in God's eyes. Unfortunately, your child will probably experience it at some time during his childhood. He may be persecuted by:

- the class bully,
- the older child down the street,
- the ringleader of the gang,
- the rebel, or
- the relentless tease.

We all know such children and we all know that they seem to have no capacity for mercy. Sometimes the persecution comes in the form of ridicule. It may be manifested as rejection. It may come in the form of teasing.

As you teach your child to pray for those who are persecuting her, teach your child that Jesus, who hears your child's prayer, knows what it means to be persecuted. He was persecuted to the point of death! He understands how your child feels.

> *Thank you, Jesus, for knowing how I feel when other people persecute me. Help me to be able to take whatever they dish out and to respond as You would.*

Encourage your child to ask the Lord for wisdom about how to respond to persecution.

> *Please show me, heavenly Father, what I should do. How should I talk to this person? Should I ignore him? Should I try to be friends with him? What is the right thing to say?*

Turning the other cheek, facing persecution, praying for those who hurt you are all tough things to do at any age. What a valuable reward is promised, however, to those who do. They will be called the sons and daughters of God.

35 • Thank God for Sending Jesus

The next day John saw Jesus coming toward him, and said, "Behold! The Lamb of God who takes away the sin of the world!
—John 1:29

"Why did Jesus come to the earth?" That's a good question to discuss with your children. Explain to your child that Jesus came to show us what God is like and to show us how to live in a way that is pleasing to God. Talk about incidents in the life of Jesus that reveal various traits of God, that show us how to respond in certain situations, and that show the love of God extended toward us.

Jesus showed us that God:

• *Wants us to be whole in body, mind, spirit, and emotions.* Time and again, Jesus said to people, "Be thou made whole." Encourage your child to ask God for wholeness.

> *Heavenly Father, please make me whole. You know the parts of my life where I am weak or unable to do certain things. Please give me Your strength in those areas. Make me whole.*

• *Wants us to live with Him forever.* That is the very reason that Jesus died on the Cross. He became the supreme sacrifice for sin so that we won't have to die for our sins.

> *Heavenly Father, thank you that you want me to live with You always in Heaven.*

This fact truly hit home to a dear family friend, Amy, when she was with us one year at the Garden Tomb in Jerusalem. It was Amy's first visit to Israel, and as she walked out of the empty tomb she was deeply moved. "He's really alive!" she said.

• *Wants us to love one another.* Jesus continually taught that it was God's desire that we love one another, do good one to another, pray for one another, and build one another up so that we can all grow to be more like Him.

> *Help me, heavenly Father, to grow up to think and talk and act like Jesus, Your Son. I want to be more and more like Him—and like You—every day.*

Encourage your child to thank God for sending Jesus every time he hears a Bible story about Jesus, and every time he has a new spiritual insight into the life of the Lord. Encourage your child to thank Him for the lessons that He continues to teach us day by day as we obey His Word.

36 • Include Your Child in Prayer Meetings

Jesus said, "Let the little children come to Me, and do not forbid them; for of such is the kingdom of heaven.
—Matthew 19:14

Include your child in your prayer meetings and church services. Don't send him away to another room to play or to be entertained. Don't exclude her from the presence of the Lord. That's what Jesus's disciples tried to do to the children one day and Jesus soundly rebuked them. "Let them come," said Jesus. "Don't forbid them. Give them the opportunity to be in My presence and to experience who I am!"

Children learn by watching others and then copying them. Let your child learn how to pray by watching you pray. Give your child an opportunity to experiment and to "try out" prayer.

Your child may not feel much boldness in the Lord. Your child may not feel like saying anything. Still, allow your child the freedom to be a part of your prayer meeting and to pray to the extent that he or she *wants* to pray.

Often, children are just comfortable "being" in a room where prayer is happening. In fact, they may relax so much that they go to sleep. Let that happen! Our grandchildren have been in three-hour home prayer meetings all their lives. They're entirely comfortable sitting for a while, climbing up on the lap of this one and that one, lying on the floor, sometimes praying, sometimes watching, sometimes dozing. Give your child the freedom to move around during a prayer meeting, to shift positions, to stand for a while, and to sit for a while. Let her relax in the Lord's presence and feel comfortable, yet reverent, in His throne-room.

Tell your child in advance what you expect of him during the meeting. Let him know the limits you will place on his behavior before the meeting begins.

The Bible does not prescribe a set position for prayer. Some people in the Bible prayed standing up, others were prostrate on their faces before God. Some kneeled; some prayed as they walked; some lifted up holy hands. Give your child the freedom of position that Bible people enjoyed. Let your child stand or sit or move about as he prays.

You can help train your child to take part in group prayer meetings. Give your child the freedom to add an "amen" to any other person's prayer with which he agrees. Or ask him to pray just one word of thanksgiving during a family prayer meeting, a word such as *safety* or *friends*. Move, next, to one sentence from each person in your family or small-group prayer meeting.

Thank you that I got to play with Jenny today.

Thank you that we got to have pizza for dinner.

Let the children come. Jesus did.

37 • Pray Aloud

Jesus lifted up His eyes and said, "Father, I thank You that You have heard Me."
—John 11:41

Prayer is *voicing* our petitions to the Lord. Praise is *declaring* the wonderful and mighty deeds of the Lord to the earth.

Petitioning is asking things of God. This is the way that God chose for us to communicate with Him, so that in His love, He can answer our requests.

When we pray silently, our prayer is heard in heaven and recorded there as all of our thoughts are. But, when we want something done on earth, we should ask aloud with all our heart. Teach your child to pray aloud.

Two things happen when a person prays aloud. First, the person who is praying is also listening. He is hearing his own voice. He's hearing his own petitions. Second, very often we don't really know what we think about a matter until we start talking about it. Sometimes we are surprised at what comes out of our own mouths. That happens in prayer, too. The Holy Spirit guides our prayer and leads us to pray in ways that we may not have initially thought or planned to pray.

Jesus said, "Whatever you *ask* in prayer, believing, you will receive" (Matt. 21:22). Ask verbally. Teach your child to voice his concerns, to speak out of his feelings, to lift up his voice in praise to God.

From the time our children were born again (during

their elementary school years), I wouldn't let more than three days go by without hearing them pray. I'd let them get by with silent prayers or "I don't want to pray" responses for no longer than three days, and then I canceled all my plans, and theirs. We would spend a delightful time together talking about the wonderful ways of Jesus. By the time evening had come, their personal relationship with the Lord was renewed so that they would again be eager to pray aloud. I knew if they went longer than three days, something was amiss in their lives—their prayers were a barometer of their relationship with the Lord. If a child is in the habit of praying aloud, his sudden refusal to pray aloud can be a clear indication of a problem he is experiencing or of something that is troubling him spiritually.

Insist that your child pray aloud. Pray aloud in your child's presence. In so doing, you'll reveal your souls to one another and enter into new levels of communication that are the richest and dearest you'll ever know.

38 • Pray During the Storms of Life

O Lord God of hosts,
Who is mighty like You, O Lord?
Your faithfulness also surrounds You.
You rule the raging of the sea;
When its waves rise, You still them.
                          —Psalm 89:8–9

You do not need to stop what you are doing in order to pray. Pray as you do, pray as you go, pray as you move.

This is an important lesson to teach your children when they feel threatened by powerful forces coming against them. Panic paralyzes. Prayer frees.

When our children were in junior high, a raging fire threatened the neighborhood where we lived. The weather had been extremely dry and the grasses were just like tinder in both of the canyons on either side of our house. When fire broke out, it spread quickly, burning many houses in its path.

One of my most vivid scenes of this entire afternoon was seeing my daughter LeeAnn running for water, her arms waving an empty water bucket and praying loudly against the fire as it moved ever closer to the neighbors' yard. Bucket after bucket after bucket of water was carried in prayer, all of us beseeching the Lord to stop the fire before it damaged the home of our neighbors, fellow Christians.

The winds changed direction that afternoon, blowing the fire back into itself. Although the grasses had charred themselves all the way to our neighbors' fence, their yard had no damage. The fire did not cross the road. Our property was spared. We felt as David must have felt when he declared in song, "He is my refuge and my fortress;/My God, in Him I will trust./Surely He shall deliver you from the snare of the fowler/And from the perilous pestilence" (Ps. 91:2–3).

- When lightning flashes and the thunder rolls, pray even as you take refuge from the storm!
- When the ship tosses on the storm sea, pray even as you batten down the hatches and tighten your life vest!
- When the hurricane blows with its fury toward your home, pray even as you board up the windows!

No matter what the terror that is lashing out at you—pray!

*O God, save us now! Hosanna!**

---

* *Hosanna* is actually a prayer which means "Lord, save us now."

39 • Pray in Times of Death

Now may our Lord Jesus Christ Himself, and our God and Father, who has loved us and given us everlasting consolation and good hope by grace, comfort your hearts and establish you in every good word and work.

—2 Thessalonians 2:16–17

Death is a part of life, even the lives of many children. Grieving and sorrow are a part of death, and thus, of life. Prayer can bring healing for the grief-stricken heart of a child.

• Talk about heaven and eternity with your child. Describe heaven in concrete terms. Anticipate what life in heaven will be like. Pray to live so that you will go to heaven when you die.

> *Thank you, heavenly Father, that I can live with You someday in heaven. You are the Giver of Life and have all control over death. I look forward to being with You in that safe, happy place You are preparing for me.*

• Assure your child that it's OK to feel sad and to cry. Even Jesus cried at the tomb of his friend Lazarus.

Heavenly Father, You see my heart and You know how sad I am that I can't be with this person that I love. Please heal this ache in my heart.

- Assure your child of God's protection over his life. When he feels weak and vulnerable, turn his thoughts to prayer.

    Heavenly Father, thank You that You are always there. Please provide everything that we need—the money to pay our bills, a place to live, enough food to eat. I trust You to take care of us.

- Discuss with your child the unfathomable wisdom of God. There is no understanding the why's of death. God has a reason that we don't know and can't know in the midst of our grief.

    Heavenly Father, we can't begin to know all of Your reasons for the things that happen to us, including the time of our death. Help us to accept the fact of this loved one's death as part of Your wisdom and love. We trust You with our life and with our death.

40 • Pray for Help in the New Place

Do not fear, little flock, for it is your Father's good pleasure to give you the kingdom.
—Luke 12:32

Your child may face a number of new situations, new challenges, new environments as he grows up:

- the new house and neighborhood;
- the first trip to camp;
- the new school or teacher;
- the new church and Sunday school class; or
- the first part-time job.

Prayer can help ease the transition from the old and familiar to the new and scary.

Pray for and with your child to have courage. Give your child some people-meeting skills. Encourage your child to make the first move, "Hi, my name is [name]. What's yours?" Prepare your child with some conversation-starting questions.

Thank you, heavenly Father, for going with me into this new setting. I trust You to be by my side and to help me to look people right in the eye and introduce myself and to not be scared.

Pray for and with your child to be a giver in the new setting. Express to your child how much he has to offer to the new situation or setting. Encourage your child to look for opportunities to give to others in the new setting.

Heavenly Father, help me to be brave as I meet new people. Help me to see ways in which I can help them. They may be just as scared as I am. Help me to be a friend to them.

Pray that your child will be alert in his new surroundings. A new environment or setting can sometimes be so overwhelming that it "freezes" a child. Prepare your child as much as you can in advance of the day when she goes into the new setting by telling her as much as you know about the new school, the camp, the job, the neighborhood. Give your child as much advance information as you can.

Heavenly Father, help me to see everything that is interesting and beautiful in this new place. Don't let me be so scared that I become afraid to explore.

As your child leaves you to embark on his journey into the unknown setting, pray even as you hug him goodbye,

Thank you, Lord Jesus, that You are going with my child and that You will be with him every second of this day and every day in this place. Help him to do his best and to be a witness for You.

Assure your child that Jesus understands what it's like to face a new situation or enter a new place. After all, as just a toddler, he moved to a foreign land, and then a few years later, moved again to a place he didn't know. He encountered new people and new situations His entire life.

Thank you, Lord Jesus, that You know exactly what I'm facing and how I'm feeling because You've felt this way, too.

Give your child directions about how he can get back home to you. It may be via a quarter and a phone number tucked into a pocket. It may be a little map that he helps to prepare. Assure your child that he can reach you in an emergency. At the same time, assure your child that he is never out of the heavenly Father's sight.

Thank you, heavenly Father, that You know all about this new place and You are there with me always!

41 ● Pray for Courage to Stand Up to Peer Pressure

Behave courageously, and the Lord will be with the good.

—2 Chronicles 19:11

Your child is going to face temptation. It may be:

- smoking,
- drinking,
- using drugs,
- looking at pornographic magazines,
- telling dirty jokes,
- going to a bad movie,
- engaging in sexual activities,
- watching a horror video,
- shoplifting,
- any other form of sin.

Prepare your child in advance. Turn the popular just-say-no campaign slogan into a prayer:

Lord, help me to say no!

Children need to be taught that they have both the authority and the ability to say "No" to any form of evil, temptation, or lie. They do not need to play along, play dumb, or play with fire.

Children have the *authority* to say no because the One whom they are ultimately trying to please is their heavenly Father. Friends are fun to have. It's nice to be noticed and included by peers. But their standards may not be God's.

Children have the *ability* to say no because the Holy Spirit said He would give them that ability any time they called upon Him for help.

> *Thank you, heavenly Father, for sending the Holy Spirit to help me right* now. *Give me the courage to say "No." Show me what is right to do. Give me the courage to do what You show me to do.*

The number one taunt of children who are trying to pressure another child into sin or misbehavior is this: "Oh, you're just too scared." Teach your child to say, "No, I'm smart. I'm smart enough to know right from wrong. I'm smart enough to know what's good for me and what isn't." Every child needs the assurance that it is OK to say "No," even if he is the only child in the group that does so.

Assure your child that it's not a sin to feel temptation, only to give in to it. Even the Lord Jesus was tempted.

Encourage your child to pray for friends who want to

be like Jesus and who don't want to engage in sinful, harmful activities.

Heavenly Father, please send me friends who love You and who want to do what is right in Your eyes.

42 • Pray for Courage to Take a Stand When the Lord's Name Is Taken in Vain

Be of good courage,
And he shall strengthen your heart,
All you who hope in the Lord.
—Psalm 31:24

Every child I have ever met faces a moment when a friend or acquaintance takes the Lord's name in vain, using it as a byword or a curse word.

Your child will no doubt cringe when that happens. A child who has been taught to respect and love his heavenly Father and the Lord Jesus will want to flee from the presence of someone who doesn't show equal respect and love. What can your child do in these instances?

First, he can pray for courage to take a stand. This is not a time to remain quietly on the sidelines. You may want to teach your child some lines to use, such as "I know that Person you just mentioned. Do you know Him, too?" Or, "I pray to Him. Do you pray to Him, too?" Or, "You just called on His name? What are you wanting Him to do for you?" Encourage your child to pray for boldness:

> *Heavenly Father, help me to be bold right now and to take a stand. Show me exactly what to say to this person. Help me to show love and concern, not hate and ridicule.*

Second, your child can walk away rather than stay in the presence of the offending person. He should not enter into a debate or a fight with him. Often, the person who has taken the Lord's name in vain is embarrassed when challenged. He may turn to vent his anger or ridicule toward your child. Your child does not need to stand and hear that. Walking away takes courage and restraint.

Explain to your child, however, that his encounter with such a person may lead that person to change his life and start following the Lord. The person may not know that his language is offensive to God because he has heard it so often in his environment. Teach your child to pray,

> *Heavenly Father, seal my ears from this abuse and help me not to strike back. Cause my stand for You to bring this person into a new relationship with*

*You so they will love You and not use Your name as
a curse word.*

What should you do when your child tries out curse
words that he hears? Punish him just as you would for
his breaking any other of the Ten Commandments. Remind your child that the Lord has said, "You shall not
take the name of the Lord your God in vain, for the
Lord will not hold him guiltless who takes His name in
vain" (Ex. 20:7).

Let your child know that you consider cursing to be a
serious offense against God and you and your family.
Let your child know that the Lord is offended by what
your child has said. Encourage your child to pray,

*Heavenly Father, I'm sorry about what I have said
against You and your Son, Jesus. Please forgive me
and help me never to say that again.*

Remind your child that it is a high privilege to use the
name of the Lord for *good* purposes, a privilege that is
never to be abused.

43 • Pray for Protection Against Evil in the Media

For you, O Lord, will bless the righteous;
With favor You will surround him as with a
shield.

—Psalm 5:12

Children are bombarded with evil messages today, a fact that is generally underestimated by many parents. Watch an hour of "children's television" in the afternoon, a program intended for after-school viewing by your child. (If you are at work when these programs are aired, videotape them for viewing at your convenience.)

As you watch the programs, look for acts of violence, signs of the occult, and titillating overtones.

Take in the latest advertised "children's movie"— without your child! Listen to the language used in the movie and evaluate the values portrayed.

Billboards . . . radio . . . magazine covers . . . just about everywhere your child turns, he is going to be exposed to images that you would like for him not to see. Here is what you and your child can do.

- *Pray* that these images will not lodge in your child's mind or invade his dreams. Pray with your child nightly,

   Cleanse my mind, Lord. Wipe out any thought or image that You don't want there.

- *Pray* that your child will not even see or hear many of the messages being hurled his way, that he will experience a protection of the saving blood of Jesus over all of his senses. Ask the Lord to blind your child from evil.

   Heavenly Father, keep me from seeing and hearing evil today. Guard my eyes and ears. Protect me from anything that would lead me to put my trust in magic instead of in You, Lord Jesus.

- *Pray* that your child will have a tender conscience. Pray that the Holy Spirit will prick his heart every time he is exposed to evil so that he will turn away from it and turn toward the Lord. Pray with your child,

   Lord Jesus, give my child a heart that is sensitive to You. Give him courage to turn off the television set or the music when the words or pictures are ones that he knows are not pleasing to You.

Praying with and for your child in this manner and encouraging your child to pray against evil does three things.

First, your child will gain confidence that he *can* withstand evil. Second, your child's conscience will remain tender toward the Lord. Third, your child will develop an awareness of his own future in the Lord.

44 • Pray for Comfort in Times of Suffering

Keep me as the apple of Your eye;
Hide me under the shadow of Your wings,
From the wicked who oppress me,
From my deadly enemies who surround me.
—Psalm 17:8–9

In every direction you look today, you will find suffering children. Some are suffering from physical, emotional, or sexual abuse. Others are suffering from addiction, AIDS, leukemia, and other major illnesses. Vast numbers of the world's children are suffering from malnutrition or the effects of war. Although many helps of a practical nature, including counseling and medical assistance, are both appropriate and necessary to lessen the impact of these problems, we can also take comfort in the fact that prayer eases suffering. Teach your child to say no to abuse, to stand up to it, to run away from it, and to always tell you of any abusive behavior they experience or witness.

Heavenly Father, help me to recognize when people are out to do me harm and to have the courage to run away from them. If someone I love hurts me without cause, help me to stand up to them in the name of Jesus or to tell someone I trust about their words and actions.

Assure the child that no abuse or rejection is beyond the understanding and compassion of Jesus. He paid the price so that we can be free of any lingering hurts.

Thank you, Lord Jesus, for taking upon Yourself this hurt that has come against my life. Praise to You, Lord Christ, for dying on the Cross so that I can be free forever of any guilt, harm, or hate that the devil would try to put on me.

• Do you know a child who is suffering with a disease? Tenderly comfort that child and pray with him,

Help me, Lord Jesus. Take away my pain. Take away my suffering. Take this disease from my body. Fill me with Your healing presence. Give me the strength to endure.

• Do you know a child who is hurting because his parents are going through a separation or divorce? Assure him that this action is not his fault, nor is it God's doing.

Help me, Lord Jesus, to feel Your love. Help me not to become bitter. Keep hatred out of my heart. Heal the hurt that I feel. Help me trust You with my future.

• Do you know a child who has suffered from the news or actual assault of war? Pray with him.

Heavenly Father, please drive the images of war from my mind. Don't let them linger in my memories. Heal me from the fear that I have felt. Help me to put my trust in You. Help me to face the future with hope.

Intercede for your child. Pray daily that your child will be spared the abuse and suffering of this world. Teach your child to pray on a daily basis:

Let me hide away in you, O Lord. Cover me with your protecting feathers the way a hen covers her chicks. Be my shield against harm. Restore my soul.

45 ● Pray as You Read the Bible

Teach me Your way, O Lord,
And lead me in a smooth path.
—Psalm 27:11

As you read the Bible with your child—or as your child reads the Bible for herself—encourage your child to include prayer as a part of her devotional time. Teach your child to pray in direct response to the Scriptures.

Before you read a Bible story, or before your child reads the Bible, pray,

> *Help me, heavenly Father, to understand what I am about to read. Give me new insights into Your Word and into Your will for my life. Let me see ways in which I can apply what I am about to read to my daily life.*

Encourage your child to read the Bible aloud to herself. She will get more out of it if she *hears* it read, even if the voice is her own. Children are excited about their own ability to read the Bible.

Teach your child to pray before or after he reads the Word aloud:

> *What I am reading I consider to be a prayer to You, O Lord.*

For example, if your child is reading Psalm 8:1—"O Lord, our Lord,/How excellent is Your name in all the earth,/You who set Your glory above the heavens!"—let your child stop and say,

> *That's my prayer, too, Lord! Your name is excellent. Your glory is higher than the skies. Receive this as my praise to You.*

After you finish a time of Bible reading, pray with your child or teach him to pray,

> *Hide this word away in my mind, heavenly Father. Don't let me forget what I have read. Help me to remember it always. Cause the Holy Spirit to remind me of this passage of Scripture at any time I need to remember it and apply it to my life.*

Many children today are becoming adept at using computers. They understand computer terms and concepts. Encourage your child to memorize passages of Scripture, especially prayers and promises, and then, to pray,

> *Heavenly Father, please file this passage of Scripture on the hard disk of my soul and cause it to come up on the screen of my mind whenever I need it.*

As your child encounters various circumstances and situations in life, encourage him to remind the Lord of

His promises and to recall the Word of the Lord. Teach your child to pray,

> *I ask you boldly to act on that Word of Yours right now, on my behalf. I know that because it is Your Word, I am praying in Your will so I pray as Jesus taught us to pray, Thy will be done on earth—right now—as it is in heaven.*

As your child covers his Bible reading with prayer in this way, the concepts of the Bible and the principles of God are reinforced in his life. The Bible comes more alive to your child, and more applicable. Praying the Scriptures builds your child's faith.

46 • Pray for Courage to Tell the Truth

Teach me good judgment and knowledge,
For I believe Your commandments.
Before I was afflicted I went astray,
But now I keep Your word.
—Psalm 119:66–67

Children lie. Much of their capacity to lie stems from the fact that they have no inborn capacity to differentiate between the concrete world and the world of their imaginations. Fantasy is real to them. Our goal as parents is to confront our children continually—often repeatedly on one subject—with reality and its consequences.

Lying comes in several forms: not telling the whole truth, telling more than the truth (exaggeration), and blatant untruths intended to distort or deceive. All types of lies need to be challenged.

Assure your child that he doesn't need to use lies. Children often tell lies to cover up another sin. Let your child know that there's nothing he has done that is beyond the forgiveness of God. He can speak the truth, repent of his deed, and be forgiven. There's no need to compound a situation with a lie.

Point your child toward prayer when he lies.

Heavenly Father, I'm sorry that I lied. Please forgive me. I know that it was wrong for me to lie. Help me not to lie again.

When you sense your child falling into deception, confront it together in prayer:

Heavenly Father, we want to live in the light of your Truth. Help us to know Your truth. We don't want to be living a lie or to be tricked by deception.

Finally, recognize that lying can easily become a habit. Lying allows a child to manipulate others. Having power over others can be enjoyable for a child, who often feels he has no power over anything. As a result, he lies repeatedly in order to have that temporarily satisfying feeling that comes from having power or "winning" over another person. Confront this attitude in your child any time you encounter it. Don't let your child get away with lying. Encourage your child to pray,

Heavenly Father, help me to develop a desire to tell the truth. Help me to not want to lie. Help me to be able to tell the difference between a lie and the truth.

47 • Pray with Persistence

Then Jesus spoke a parable to them, that men always ought to pray and not lose heart.
—Luke 18:1

Read Luke 18:1–8. The widow in Jesus' parable never gave up. Jesus uses her example as a means of teaching us that we should never give up in our prayers, either. Pray until:

- *You know God's answer.* If you have a question about something, ask God for wisdom. Pray until you receive it. Declare to the Lord,

  I'm not doing anything until You show me what to do. I'm not going to make a decision without knowing that it's the right one in Your eyes.

- *You see the change for good that you want in your life.* Encourage your child to pray for traits that Jesus exhibited in His life. If your child has a tendency to steal, have your child pray daily,

  Help me, heavenly Father, not to steal. Convict me in my heart every time I'm about to take something that isn't mine. Give me the courage not to steal. I don't want to be a thief, Lord. Help me not to be!

By praying daily about a character trait such as this, your child is actually causing his own mind, through prayer, to become more like the mind of Jesus.

- *You either see the miracle you desire, or God takes the desire for something out of your heart.* Pray before you intercede for another person,

   Heavenly Father, I want to pray in Your will. This is my desire. If that isn't Your desire, show me that it isn't.

We insisted that our children be persistent in prayer in two ways.

First, we made certain that our children prayed daily to *"grow in the grace and knowledge of the Lord."*

Second, we insisted that our children pray daily that they might *"be a blessing and not a hindrance"* to the good things that God wanted to do in their lives.

The more times your child prays for or about something, the more important it becomes to him, the more value he places on it, the more vital it is to his life.

48 • Pray Knowing That Jesus Hears You

And Jesus called a little child to Him, set him in the midst of them, and said, "Assuredly, I say to you, unless you are converted and become as little children, you will by no means enter the kingdom of heaven.

—Matthew 18:2–3

Your child is important to God. Your child has God's ear. In fact, Jesus taught that it is a prerequisite for us *all* to become as little children in our level of faith, trust, adoration, and obedience if we are truly to enter the kingdom of heaven.

Assure your child that Jesus hears his praise. The psalmist challenged us, "Oh, clap your hands, all you peoples! Shout to God with the voice of triumph!" (Ps. 47:1). *All you peoples*—your child certainly is included in that group!

Assure your child that Jesus hears your child's petitions. Your child is as valuable to him as any adult. His needs are important to the Lord.

Assure your child that God hears even his whispers. God isn't hard of hearing. God also pays attention—full, undivided attention—to your child when he prays. Children often live in environments where they are mostly overlooked or their words are ignored.

Assure your child that whenever he calls upon the name of the Lord, he has the Lord's complete and undivided attention. The Lord hears his prayer loud and clear. Furthermore, the Lord understands his prayer, even if he doesn't use adult words. The Lord will not stifle or say "Shhh" to your child's petition.

When you assure your child that the Lord hears, understands, and *desires* his prayers, you are building your child's confidence that God will act on your child's prayers. We are to know a fullness of "joy and peace in believing" (Rom. 15:13). That won't happen for your child unless he first believes that the heavenly Father is hearing him when he prays and that He understands what your child is attempting to say. Give your child that assurance.

Lead your child in thanksgiving,

> *Thank you, heavenly Father, that You hear my prayers! Thank you that You understand me completely and You know what I'm saying. Thank you that You know how to answer my prayer with the very best answer!*

49 • Pray for a Loving and Understanding Heart

When He saw the multitudes, He was moved with compassion for them, because they were weary and scattered, like sheep having no shepherd.

—Matthew 9:36

A spirit of criticism seems to have the Christian world in its grip. Such a spirit robs the *criticizer* far more than the *criticized* because it diminishes in the criticizer a basic sense of "goodness" about the world. It destroys confidence one might place in others and, ultimately, confidence in oneself to live a blameless life above reproach (which is what we are called to do in Christ Jesus).

Encourage your child to look for good in others and to have a loving and understanding heart. Pray with your child,

Heavenly Father, establish in me the ability to see good in other people and to forgive their mistakes. Let me see others as You see them. Give me Your love for them.

Train your child to have compassion. Point out that the positive far outweighs the negative. Encourage your child to edify and build up others. Establish that concept in prayer.

Heavenly Father, I pray today for [names]. I ask You to forgive them their sins, make them whole in every area of their beings, and cause them to be filled with Your Holy Spirit so that they will bear the fruit of the Spirit. Help me to see ways in which I can help them to grow in You and to become all that You want them to be.

In building up others, your child can share his time, prayers, enthusiasm, and ideas. In lifting up others, your child can befriend them, listen to them, and pray with them. Pray with your child,

Show me, heavenly Father, a way in which I can be a blessing to my friend. Help me to do what You show me to do.

Encourage your child to pray for compassion for others, the foremost trait that Jesus exhibited as He ministered to the needs of the people.

• Pray with your child,

Help me, heavenly Father, to be courteous to others.

• Pray with your child,

> *Help me, heavenly Father, not to return evil for*
> *evil. Help me not to strike back or try to get even.*
> *Help me to plant good seeds even if other people*
> *are planting bad ones.*

• Pray with your child,

> *Help me, heavenly Father, not to talk bad about*
> *another person. Help me not to spread rumors or*
> *to talk back in an angry way to people. Help me to*
> *speak kind words even if others speak bad ones.*

Praying for compassion causes a child's empathy for others to grow, and it will keep your child's heart tender and soft toward the Lord and toward others.

50 • Your Prayer Can Be a Song

Be filled with the Spirit, speaking to one another in psalms and hymns and spiritual songs, singing and making melody in your heart to the Lord, giving thanks always for all things to God the Father in the name of our Lord Jesus Christ.

—Ephesians 5:18–20

When our children were teenagers, one year we sang prayers and praise to the Lord in the orchard. We simply made up songs out of our hearts, creating tunes to go with the words we wanted to say to the Lord.

Encourage your child to make up "spiritual songs" that come from the depth of his own being. Make up the words. They don't need to rhyme. Make up the tunes. They don't need to be in perfect rhythm. Let these songs be freewheeling ones that convey meaning and feeling, without regard to perfection of form.

- Sing songs of *praise,* listing the magnificent deeds of God to you, your child, and to others you know.
- Sing songs of *thanksgiving,* citing the many ways in which you are thankful to the Lord for who He is to you and for what He has done on your behalf.
- Sing songs of *worship,* identifying the traits of God and all that He is to you and to your child.

Sing with lifted voice. As you sing, feel free to dance, too! As Psalm 149:2 says, "Let them praise His name with the dance."

You can also encourage your child to sing songs that he already knows—choruses, praise songs, hymns— and to dedicate them to the Lord. Your child can simply say to the Lord,

Heavenly Father, this song is for You.

Give your child the privilege of singing to the Lord as if he was singing to you or to any other person in the room.

Encourage your child to accompany his singing with instruments and clapping. The psalmist did.

Prayer and praise that is framed in song gives your child an opportunity for free-form worship before the Lord. This will acquaint him with the emotion of loving Jesus and of feeling His love envelope and permeate him.

51 • Pray That the Lord Will Give You a Clean Heart

Create in me a clean heart, O God,
And renew a steadfast spirit within me.
—Psalm 51:10

Having a clean heart comes about when your child is forgiven for sin. When your child repents and asks for God's forgiveness, he *is* forgiven. That's the promise of the Lord. Assure your child of that promise.

Obedience is daily. Repentance for acts of disobedience also needs to be daily. Encourage your child to pray:

Heavenly Father, please forgive me for the things that I knew I was supposed to do today and didn't do. Help me to have the courage and the desire to do them tomorrow.

Heavenly Father, please forgive me for the things that I said or did today that made Your heart sad.

Heavenly Father, please forgive me today for disobeying.

*Heavenly Father, please forgive me for the thing that
I did today that I'm sorry I did.*

After your child asks forgiveness of you, make certain that he hears you say that you do, indeed, forgive him. After your child asks forgiveness of the Lord, assure your child that according to God's promises in the Bible, he *is* forgiven by the Lord (1 John 1:9).

Let your child hear you, too, pray for forgiveness. Let Him know that you make mistakes, too. Don't let your child grow up thinking that you, or any other adult, is perfect. A prayer for forgiveness helps assure your child that no sin he commits needs to be "covered up" in order for him to appear perfect before you, others, or the Lord.

A daily prayer for forgiveness:

- Keeps your child free from the burden of guilt.
- Creates a feeling of freedom in your child.
- Causes joy to flood your child's heart.
- Creates an environment for peaceful soul-sleep.
- Eases tension in your home.
- And builds up your child's sense of self-worth and personal value.

Make it a habit to pray daily for forgiveness!

52 • Pray That the Future Will Be Better Than Today

To them God willed to make known what are the riches of the glory of this mystery among the Gentiles: which is Christ in you, the hope of glory.

—Colossians 1:27

Assure your child that the best is yet to come. No matter what the trials, struggles, hardships, or challenges of today, God is there with her now, and He will continue to be there to bring victory out of seeming defeat. Assure your child that you believe with your whole heart that God will make a way for your child, that she will have everything she needs in this life and that she will enjoy eternal life with the Lord in heaven after she dies. What a future!

Talk to your child about what it means to have abundance—spiritually, emotionally, mentally, materially. Point out the generosity of God's blessings to us, the unending flow of good things that He desires for us to have, know, feel, and experience.

• Praise the Lord for your child's future and all the good things that are yet to come.

- Praise the Lord for the family that your child will have one day.
- Praise the Lord for the work that your child will do and for the contribution he will make to his church, community, and nation.
- Praise the Lord for the souls that your child is going to win to the Lord during her life.
- Praise the Lord for the blessing that your child is going to be to others as he prays for them, encourages them, builds them up, loves them, and blesses them in the Name of Jesus.
- Praise the Lord for the spiritual battles that your child is going to win—against the devil and for the advancement of the kingdom of God.
- Praise the Lord for the heavenly home that awaits us, where we will all be able to live together forever and ever with those we love.

Yes, praise the Lord! And even as you praise Him with your child, assure your child that as great as your hopes are for the future, and as good as you envision God's future blessings to be, your hopes and dreams are only a fraction of the hopes and dreams that God has for your child.